Adventure in Rome

I Talk You Talk Press

CONTENTS

CHAPTER ONE

Lily was happy. She was in Rome for a week. She was on a package tour. The group of tourists arrived at the airport, and got on the bus. The guide was a young woman called Bianca.

Bianca said, "We will now go to the hotel. We are staying near Piazza Navona. It is a beautiful area."

Lily looked around the bus. All of the other tour members were older than her. Lily was thirty-one. The other tour members were all retired. Usually, she didn't like package tours. She liked to travel alone. But her mother wanted to go on vacation with her this year. So, they booked a package tour to Rome. Then, something bad happened. The day before the package tour, her mother fell over in the garden. It was not a big accident, but she hurt her foot, so she couldn't walk very well.

Lily wanted to cancel the package tour, but her mother said, 'We won't get the money back. You go.' So, Lily went alone.

Lily looked around the bus.

I don't like package tours, she thought. *I like travelling alone, and going to bars. I will stay at the hotel and eat with everyone. I will go on some sightseeing trips too, but I will try to spend some time alone.*

She looked out of the window as the bus drove through the streets of Rome.

This is very different to Dublin, she thought. *I think I will enjoy my time here.*

Bianca made an announcement.

"Everyone. Please listen to me. I will now give you a pink badge. You must wear this badge all the time. It is the tour group badge."

Bianca gave everyone the badges.

"Do I have to wear it too?" asked Lily. *I don't need a badge. I won't get lost!* she thought.

"Yes, it is a rule. Everyone must wear the badge," said Bianca.

"OK," said Lily. She put it on her jacket.

The bus stopped on a busy road.

"We will walk to the hotel door," said Bianca. "It is in a very narrow street, and the bus cannot drive down it."

Lily got off the bus and looked around.

The buildings are so old and beautiful! she thought.

They walked around the corner into one of the many narrow streets. There were cars parked on one side of the road. The hotel was an old building.

I will enjoy staying here, thought Lily.

After check-in, Lily rested in her room until dinner. Her room was at the front of the hotel, and she could see the street and the cars below.

Dinner started at 7 o'clock. Lily sat with a couple from Dublin, called Bernard and Kelly. They enjoyed talking about life in Dublin while they ate delicious lasagna and salad. Lily drank some red wine, and enjoyed it very much.

After dinner, Lily thought, *I want to go outside and see Rome at night. I want to take some photos and videos for my blog, and to show my mother.*

She went back to her room, put her jacket on, picked up her handbag, and walked out into the night.

CHAPTER TWO

Marco and James were sitting in a car in a street near the Pantheon. It was not their car. They stole it from another city the day before. It was a dark, narrow street, with only a few lights. There were no people around. Tourists didn't come down this street.

"When he comes out of the door, I will jump out of the car and kill him with this knife," said James. He took a small knife out of his pocket. Marco felt nervous.

James is crazy, he thought. *That knife is too small.*

"Then, I will get back in the car and you will drive away very fast. Don't stop until we arrive at the house."

"OK," said Marco. "I understand."

James looked at the apartment window above.

"I told him many times to give me my money. He had many chances. Now, it is too late."

"But if you kill him, you won't get the money," said Marco.

"No, I won't. But other people owe me money too. They will pay soon when they hear about this."

He lit a cigarette.

"What are we going to do if someone comes?" asked Marco.

"No one will come. You think too much," said James.

Marco was worried. "We should wait until later."

"It's OK! Now is our chance! He knows we are looking for him. Luigi told me he is leaving Rome tonight. So this is our only chance!"

The light in the apartment went off.

"OK! He's coming! This is it!"

CHAPTER THREE

Lily was enjoying her walk around Rome. She was recording everything on her smartphone. She planned to upload the videos to YouTube, so her mother could see them.

I have a lot of video of the large busy roads, thought Lily. *Now, I'll take some video of the side streets. They are very pretty.*

She switched on the video recorder again and walked down a side street. She stopped. Two men were in front of her. The men looked at her. They looked at her smartphone. One of the men was holding something. He put it in his pocket. He ran away and jumped into a car. The car drove away very quickly. The other man looked at Lily, ran into the apartment building, and closed the door.

Lily stood in the street.

That was strange, she thought. *What were the men doing? One man looked angry and the other man looked very frightened. One man was holding something. Was it a knife? Maybe they were fighting. Well, I have a video of real life in Rome! There is more here than old buildings!*

She continued to walk down the street recording everything on her smartphone.

CHAPTER FOUR

Marco was driving very fast through the streets.

"I don't believe it! I don't believe it!" James punched the car door. "Why? Why? Why did that woman come into the street at that time? Why?"

Marco was frightened. James was a very violent person. They had been in the same gang for a long time. James had killed many people.

"I don't know, James," he said.

"Of course you don't know," said James. "You never know anything. We missed our chance! Now Tom knows we are looking for him, and we want to kill him! But it is worse than that! That woman was recording everything on her smartphone! She looked young. Young people these days post videos on Facebook or YouTube. Everyone will see it! We have to find that woman before she can upload the video."

"But how can we find her? There are millions of tourists in Rome!" said Marco.

James was quiet for a few seconds. Then, he said, "She was wearing a pink badge. I think it was the badge of a tour group. So if we can find the tour group name, we can find the hotel. Then, we can find her. We must get her smartphone, before it is too late!"

"How are we going to find the tour group?" asked Marco.

"I don't know. Let's think," said James.

Then, Marco said, "I have an idea. Luigi's girlfriend, Anna, works at a travel agency. We could ask her to find out for us."

James smiled. "Good thinking Marco! Good thinking!"

He picked up his phone and called Luigi.

CHAPTER FIVE

Lily had a coffee in a café in Piazza Navona, and went back to the hotel at around 10:00pm.

I'll upload the videos tomorrow, she thought. *I'm too tired to do it tonight.*

She had a bath, and then went to sleep.

The next morning, she woke up at 7:00am.

I hope the weather is nice today, she thought.

She opened the curtains. The sky was blue. There were many cars parked in the side street.

So many cars, she thought. *They are all parked very closely to each other. That will be a good photograph.*

She picked up her smartphone and leaned out of the window. She took some photographs of the cars below.

"I don't believe this!" shouted James. "There she is! In the window on the second floor! She is taking a photograph of the street! She will get a photo of our car!"

James and Marco were sitting in the stolen car in the street. Luigi's girlfriend had called many people, and found the tour group. They were a group from Ireland. They were staying in the Nice Day Hotel. She found the hotel easily. James and Marco were waiting for the group to leave the hotel. They planned to follow them, and steal Lily's smartphone. Marco was looking at his iPad.

"Look at some hashtags on Twitter and Facebook. Look for #NiceDayHotelRome," said James.

A few minutes later, Marco said, "Here it is! She has posted the photograph with the hashtag #NiceDayHotel on Twitter! Her name is Lily Keane. There is a message! It says, ---*I will upload my videos soon.---*"

"Give me the phone," said James. He looked at the photo.

"Here is the car," he said. "It's a very clear picture. Let's Google her, and see if we can find her Facebook or other accounts. We might need information about her and her family. We might need to kill them."

Kill her family? Marco was shocked, but he didn't say anything.

CHAPTER SIX

Lily and the other tour members got on the bus to go to the Colosseum. The woman sitting next to her said, "What's your name, dear?"

"I'm Lily."

"I'm Susan. Nice to meet you," said the woman.

"Pleased to meet you. Are you travelling alone?" asked Lily.

"Yes, I am. My husband died a few years ago. I travel alone a lot now. Are you alone?" asked Susan.

Lily told her about her mother's accident.

"I'm sorry to hear that," said Susan. "I hope she gets better soon."

"Thank you. I've been taking photographs and videos for her. Would you like to see them?" asked Lily.

Lily showed Susan the photographs and videos.

"This one is interesting," said Lily. "These two men were fighting I think. And then, they saw me, and one man got into a car and the other man ran inside an apartment."

Susan looked at the video and photographs. She looked worried.

"Show me that photograph of the street this morning, and the video of the men again," she said.

They watched the video again and looked at the photograph.

"That's strange," said Susan.

"What is it?" asked Lily.

"The car. The man in the video got into a black car with a white stripe on the side. The same car is in your photograph from this morning. Look."

Lily looked at the photograph. "Oh yes! You are right! How did you see that?"

Susan smiled and said, "I'm a retired police officer."

Lily laughed. "I see."

Susan did not smile. "I think it is strange. I think you should be careful," she said. "Maybe the men followed you last night."

Lily was surprised. "But why would they follow me?"

"I don't know. Maybe because you have a video of the men. Maybe because you are a pretty young girl. You should be careful."

Lily looked at the photograph again.

Maybe Susan is thinking too much. I'm sure there are many black cars with white stripes in Rome. She was a police officer, so maybe she thinks like that. I'm sure it's OK!

CHAPTER SEVEN

Luigi was walking around behind the tour group. He was trying to look like a tourist. He had a camera, and he was taking pictures.

How can I get her smartphone? She is walking in the middle of the group. She is talking to that old woman. Maybe I should wait. This is not a good place to get the phone. I cannot escape easily, he thought.

He sent a message to Marco from his phone.

---I can't get the phone in here.---

Marco replied:

---It's nearly lunch time. Go to the same restaurant. It is a nice day. They might sit outside. Try to get it then!---

Luigi thought about it. *Someone from the group might notice me in the restaurant. I'll ask Anna to have lunch with me, and I'll wear my hat and sunglasses. Maybe Anna can help me get the phone.*

He sent Anna a message.

---Meet me for lunch today. I'll tell you the name of the restaurant soon. Take a taxi. I'll pay.---

I must get the phone, thought Luigi.

Luigi was the newest member of the gang. The gang lent people money, and charged an extra fee. The leaders of the gang were Marco and James. He wanted to show the leaders he was a good gang member. Then, he could get better jobs from the gang.

If I get more money, I can take Anna on a holiday to another country. I can buy an expensive car! What car can I get? A Ferrari? A Porsche? Where can I take Anna? She has a friend in Florida. She would like to visit her, I'm sure. I could…

Suddenly, Luigi looked around. He was alone.

They've gone! he thought. *Where have they gone?*

He walked around the Colosseum quickly, but he could not find the tour group.

He saw a tour guide.

"Excuse me, that tour group, with the pink badges, where did they go?" he asked.

"They are walking back to the car park," said the guide.

"OK, thanks," said Luigi.

He ran out of the Colosseum, but he could not see them. He arrived at the car park and saw the bus. It was leaving the car park. He ran to his car and started the engine. He followed the bus out of the car park and onto the busy road.

CHAPTER EIGHT

"Well, this is a nice little restaurant," said Susan.

"Yes, it is. And it is very nice to sit outside," said Lily. "The weather is beautiful today."

A young couple came and sat down at the table next to them. The man was handsome. He was wearing a hat and sunglasses. The woman had beautiful long brown hair. She was wearing a smart office uniform.

This is a nice place for couples, thought Lily. *I wish I had a boyfriend.*

She looked at Susan. Susan looked a little upset.

"Are you OK?" asked Lily.

Susan turned to Lily and said very quietly, "That man was at the Colosseum. He was following us. I remember his pants. Jeans with red stripes on the bottoms are very unusual.

Lily looked at the man's pants. "I didn't notice the stripes," she said.

"I notice many small things. When I was a police officer…"

"Your pasta is here," said the waiter.

Susan stopped talking and they started to eat the pasta. It was delicious.

"Could I have a glass of red wine please?" asked Lily.

"Two glasses," said Susan. "I'll have a glass too."

"Certainly," said the waiter. He walked away.

Luigi was listening to their conversation.

They are drinking alcohol. Good! Maybe they will get drunk. It will be easier for me to get the phone, he thought.

After lunch, Lily stood up. "Susan, could you look after my bag, please? I'm going to the toilet."

"Sure," said Susan. "It will be safe with me."

Lily stood up and put her bag on her chair. She went into the restaurant and into the toilet. Susan finished her wine. *Should I have another glass? No, maybe I should wait for tonight. But I am on holiday, so…*

Now is my chance, thought Luigi.

He put the money on the table for the meal. Then, he and Anna stood up. He walked past the table and quickly tried to take Lily's bag.

But Susan was very quick. She stood up, and pushed Luigi. He fell over into Anna. Anna fell onto their table. All the plates and glasses fell off the table onto the ground. *SMASH!!*

Everyone looked at them. The waiters and Bianca ran over to the table.

"Are you OK? Is anybody hurt?" they asked.

"I'm sorry. I drank too much wine," said Susan. "I fell into this nice young man."

She looked at Luigi.

He is not a nice young man, she thought. *He planned to take Lily's bag.*

Lily came back from the toilet.

"Is everything OK? What happened?" she said.

"That man tried to take your bag, so I stopped him," said Susan quietly. "You must be careful. First, the car in the video and the picture. Next this. They want something. They are following you."

"But what do they want?" asked Lily.

"I think it is your phone. I think they were doing something bad that night. You have their faces on video."

Lily felt worried.

"Maybe I should go to the police," she said.

"It's too early," said Susan. "The man didn't take your bag, so the police won't do anything. Just be careful."

CHAPTER NINE

"What? A drunk old woman fell into you, and stopped you? What are you saying?" shouted James. "What are you? A man? A boy? I can't believe this!"

"I'm sorry," said Luigi. "I will try again."

"No you won't. It's too late. They know your face. This is terrible!" said Marco. "We must get that phone!"

"What are we going to do?" asked Luigi.

"Be quiet! I'm thinking!" said Marco.

They were sitting in James' luxury apartment. It had views over the hills of Rome. Marco looked out of the window. The sun was setting. The buildings of the city were golden.

"I have an idea. Lily will go out alone again. I'm sure of it. She won't want to stay in the hotel every night with the old people. James, your girlfriend Sally is visiting Rome now. She can start talking to Lily. She is from Canada, so she can say 'I'm a tourist.' She can ask Lily to go sightseeing together. Lily has many friends on Facebook, so I think she likes making new friends. They will go sightseeing together. Then, Sally can say to Lily, 'Shall I take your photograph?' Lily will trust her. Then, Sally can take the phone and run away!" said Marco.

"That's a great plan Marco!" said Luigi.

"Yes, I think it's a good idea. I'll call Sally now," said James.

15

CHAPTER TEN

It was 7:00pm. Lily wanted to go out and take some photographs and go to a café. She wanted to be alone. She walked into the hotel lobby and looked out of the window. She could not see any men or the black car.

It seems safe, she thought.

She walked out of the hotel. Sally was waiting at the corner. She started to follow Lily.

Lily walked to the river. It took 10 minutes. It was a beautiful night. There were big statues next to one of the bridges. She took out her phone and started to take some photographs.

"Excuse me," said a voice.

Lily turned around. There was a woman standing next to her.

"Could you take a photo of me please?" asked the woman.

"Sure." Lily took the camera from the woman and took a photograph.

"Are you a tourist?" asked the woman.

"Yes, I am. Are you?"

"Yes. I'm visiting from Canada. I'm Jessica," said the woman.

"I'm Lily. Nice to meet you."

They started walking along the river. They talked about their trips, and their home countries. There were many cars and bikes on the road.

"Look at all those cars," said the woman. "My home town is small. We don't have big roads like this!"

They watched the cars for a few seconds. Then, the woman said,

"Shall I take a picture of you with all the cars in the background?"

"Yes, OK," said Lily. She gave the woman her phone.

"Move a little to the right," said the woman. She held the phone up. "That's it. This will be a great photo."

She took a photograph. "I'll take one more. This time, turn around and look at the cars. Look shocked! It will be a funny photograph!" said the woman.

Lily laughed. "Sure!"

After a few seconds, she said, "Have you taken the photo?"

She turned around. The woman was gone.

CHAPTER ELEVEN

"No!" shouted Lily. "That woman has my phone!" She looked around and saw the woman running down a street. She started to chase her.

"Hey! Come back! Hey!" she shouted. Luckily, Lily was a fast runner. She caught the woman.

"Hey!" She grabbed her hair. The woman stopped and turned around. Lily punched her in the face. The woman dropped the phone.

Lily picked the phone up and ran down the street. She ran through the narrow streets. After about five minutes, she stopped. She saw a small café. She ordered a coffee and sat down. There were a few other customers.

I will be safe here, she thought.

She looked at her phone.

Susan was right, she thought. *Someone wants my phone. It must be that video. Someone wants my phone because of that video.*

She watched the video again.

I have to take this to the police. I have to tell them. When should I go to the police? Should I go now? No, it's late, and I can't speak Italian. It will be very difficult. I'll wait until tomorrow. Bianca can take me. Now, I will try to relax. Where am I? she thought. She checked the map on her phone. *I'm quite far from the hotel. About a twenty-minute walk. I will try to go back through the small streets. They are quiet, and there are not many cars. It will be easy to see any strange people.*

CHAPTER TWELVE

"I'm sorry! I tried my best!" Sally was in James' apartment with Marco, James and Luigi. She was crying.

"It's OK," said Marco.

"It's not OK!" said James, angrily. "We need to get that phone! But now that woman knows we want the phone. First Luigi tried to get it, then Sally. And you both failed!"

"She punched me!" said Sally. "My face hurts."

"I don't care!" said James. "I only care about that phone! Think about how we can get it!"

Luigi was thinking hard. He wanted to show the other men he was clever. He wanted to impress them.

"I have an idea," he said after a few minutes. "Lily was sitting with an old woman in the restaurant. We could go to the old woman's hotel room with a gun. Then, we put a note under Lily's door. On the note, we can write, 'Leave your phone on the hotel steps outside. If you don't, we will kill your friend. If you go to the police, we will kill her.' Then, we get the phone, and delete the video."

Everyone looked at Luigi. "Can you do it?" asked Sally.

"The woman is old. She is weak," said Luigi.

"She was strong enough to push you in the restaurant," said Marco.

Everyone laughed. Luigi was not happy. "That was just bad luck," he said.

"But, we don't know the woman's hotel room," said Marco.

Everyone was quiet.

"We don't know her name," said James.

"Yes, we do," said Luigi. "Her name is Susan. I remember. Lily called her Susan."

"How about this plan," said James. "Sally, you go to the hotel reception, and say to the receptionist, 'Please call Susan's room. My name is Lily. Please tell Susan I want to see her now.' The receptionist will call Susan, and Susan will say 'Yes, of course.' Then, you can ask the receptionist for the room number. When you know the room number, Marco and I will go there. Susan will open the door because she will think it is Lily. We'll keep her in the hotel room, and Luigi, you wait for Lily to put the phone on the steps."

"Great idea James! Great idea!" said Marco.

Yeah, great idea, thought Luigi. *But it was my idea too. No one says 'great idea' to me.*

"Do you know which room is Lily's?" asked Sally.

James and Marco thought hard. "We saw her leaning out of her hotel room window to take a photograph. It was on the road side of the hotel," said James. "It was the third room from the corner."

"So, why don't you just go to Lily's room? When she opens the door, show her the gun and take her phone. It is easier," said Sally.

"Because she knows something is wrong. She knows we want her phone. Maybe she has guessed why we want it, and she knows my face. She will never open the door. She'll call for help," said James. "The old woman doesn't know me or Marco. She doesn't know anything. She'll open the door and she won't scream."

"But she might scream if she sees the gun," said Sally.

"She won't. We'll tell her to keep quiet, or we will kill her," said Marco.

CHAPTER THIRTEEN

Lily went back to the hotel. No one followed her. Luigi was in a different car near the hotel entrance. He was sitting in the back seat. She didn't see him. She was tired.

I'll have a nice bath and then go to bed, she thought. She looked around the lobby carefully. *Everyone looks normal,* she thought. *No one is looking for me here.*

The elevator was empty. When she got to her floor, she looked again. The hallway was empty.

Safe, she thought. She went to her hotel room and opened the door.

There was a note on the floor of her room. She read it.

---*We have your friend, Susan. Put your phone on the steps of the hotel now. If you don't, we will kill your friend. Don't go to the police or show anyone this note. If you do, your friend will die.*---

Lily read the note again. She sat on the bed.

They have Susan! she thought. *This is terrible. What should I do? Should I go to the police? No, they might kill her. I should give them my phone. But I should keep the video. I must show the video to the police.*

Lily thought about it for a few minutes. *I can email the video to myself. Then, I can show the police later.*

Lily sent the video by email to her PC email address.

Done! she thought. *Now they can have my phone.*

She walked out of the room and got in the elevator. She walked through the lobby and outside. She looked around. She couldn't see anyone. She put her phone on the side of the steps and walked back into the hotel.

Luigi jumped out of the car and ran to the hotel steps. He picked up the phone.

I have it! I have the phone! he thought.

CHAPTER FOURTEEN

"What do you want?" said Susan. "The phone? Why couldn't you steal it? That young man in the restaurant, he was really bad. You need better gang members!"

"Shut up!" said James.

"An old woman like me! I pushed him over! He was so weak!"

"I said shut up!" James pointed a gun at Susan.

"Oh, you won't kill me," she said. "You will get the phone and get out of the hotel as quickly as you can. But I know your faces."

"I have killed people before," said James. "I can kill you easily. Shut up."

Luigi went up to Susan's room. He knocked on the door and said, "Marco! James! It's me! Open the door!"

Marco opened the door.

"I have the phone! I have the phone!" said Luigi.

"Ah, here he is! That weak boy! Are you OK? Did I hurt you in the restaurant?" asked Susan.

Luigi looked angry, but he didn't say anything.

"Give it to me," said James.

He took the phone and looked at it.

"Here! Here it is! The video! We can delete it, and then we are safe!"

Marco was thinking. Then, he said, "Give me the phone."

He looked at the phone.

"Look at this. The phone email history. A few minutes ago she sent something to her email address. I am sure it was the video."

"So just delete it," said Luigi.

"I can see the messages, but I can't delete anything from the email account without the password," said Marco.

"So what do we do?" asked Luigi. "She has the data. She can go to the police anytime."

"She won't go to the police while we have Susan," said James. The men looked at each other, and then looked at Susan.

"Call the hotel lobby. Ask to speak to Lily. Tell her to give you the password for her email address. If she says 'no', we will kill you," said James.

"I don't know the hotel number," said Susan.

Marco searched his phone. "Here it is," he said.

He called the hotel, put the speaker on, and gave Susan the phone.

"May I speak to Lily Keane please?" asked Susan.

"Wait a minute please," said the woman at the front desk.

A few seconds later, she said, "I'm sorry. There is no answer. She is not in her room."

Marco took the phone from Susan and hung up.

"She's not in her room! Where is she?" he said.

"The police! Maybe she has gone to the police!" said James. "We have to move quickly. We have to leave here."

He looked out of the window. "There is a pipe. Marco, you and I can climb down. Luigi, you stay here with the old woman. We'll go to Robert's place. Robert is good with computers. Maybe he can hack her email account."

The men went to the window.

"I don't know. That pipe doesn't look safe" said Marco.

"We have no choice. If she has gone to the police, they will be here soon," said James.

While they were talking and looking at the window, Susan was writing something on the back of a receipt. She wrote:

---*"Help! I'm in here! Danger!"*---

Then, very quickly and quietly, she pushed the paper under the door.

CHAPTER FIFTEEN

Lily ran to Bianca's room and knocked on the door.

"Bianca! Bianca! Are you there? You have to help me!" she shouted.

Bianca opened the door. She was wearing a dressing gown and was getting ready to go to bed.

"What's the matter? What is it?" she asked.

"Some men have taken Susan!" said Lily.

"Taken Susan? But why?" asked Bianca. She didn't understand.

"At night, I went out and took video of the streets on my smartphone. On one of the videos, I recorded a man. I think he had a knife. I think he planned to attack the man standing next to him. I have the video on my smartphone. The man wanted it. He and his friends tried to get my phone, but each time, they failed. Tonight they took Susan. They left a note in my room. It said, 'Give us your phone, or Susan will die.' So, I gave them my phone. But they still have Susan! We must go to the police!"

Bianca was listening carefully. "We'll call the police now," she said.

"Quickly! We don't have much time!" said Lily.

CHAPTER SIXTEEN

Ten minutes later, a policeman came into the hotel lobby. Lily and Bianca were waiting. Lily told Bianca the story. Bianca told the policeman everything in Italian.

"That sounds like James and Marco. We know them. James is very dangerous. He has killed many people. We thought he was in Southern Italy. The police there are looking for him. We didn't know he was back in Rome. We have to find them," said the policeman. "This is serious. I will call for extra policemen to come. We must find your friend."

The policeman talked on his radio to the police station.

Then Lily had an idea. She went to the reception desk.

"Did you see anyone leaving the hotel in the last hour?" she asked the receptionist.

"A woman came in and asked me to call a guest. She said her name was Lily. The guest said 'OK' so I gave her the room number. But she didn't go to the elevators. She walked out of the hotel. Then I saw you," said the receptionist. "You went out and came back very quickly. I didn't see anyone else."

"Did you see anyone come in?" asked Lily.

"Two men came in and then later another man. That's all."

"Is there any other way in and out of this hotel?" asked Lily.

"Of course," said the receptionist. "But that is for staff. You need a special key to use the staff entrance."

Lily went back to Bianca and the policeman. She told Bianca what the receptionist had said. Bianca told the policeman in Italian.

"Do you think Susan is still here?" asked Lily. "Maybe they are keeping her somewhere in the hotel."

"Maybe," said the policeman. "Let's go to her room."

Lily, Bianca and the policeman took the elevator up to Susan's floor. As they walked towards Susan's room, Lily said quietly, "Look! There is a piece of paper next to the door!"

She picked it up and read it.

---*"Help! I'm in here! Danger!"*---

"Susan is in her room!" she said.

"We need more people. I hope the extra police arrive soon," said the policeman. "I'll tell them where we are. I'll tell them to pick up a key card for this room from reception."

He talked on his radio and very soon, four more policemen with guns arrived.

Bianca and Lily watched as the policemen quietly opened the door and ran inside.

When the policemen appeared, Luigi panicked and tried to jump out of the window.

One of the policemen stopped him.

"OK Luigi. Long time no see," he said. "Tell us where James and Marco are, or you will go to prison for a long time."

Luigi was very frightened. He told the police about the phone and Robert's house.

The police put handcuffs on Luigi. Susan shook her head.

"I don't speak Italian," she said to one of the policemen. "But I think Luigi just told you everything. He is only a young boy. He is not a good gangster. Please don't be too tough with him."

When the policemen came out of Susan's room with Luigi, Lily rushed in. She ran to Susan.

"Are you OK?" Are you hurt?" she asked.

Susan laughed. "I'm OK. But poor Luigi is not," she said.

CHAPTER SEVENTEEN

Lily and Susan sat at a table outside a café. It was a beautiful sunny day.

"Our last day in Rome," said Lily. "So many things happened, I didn't really have time to see anything."

"It was an adventure. Most people come to Rome, go sightseeing, eat nice food and go home. But you and I had an adventure. It was exciting," said Susan.

Lily laughed. "Why weren't you scared? Why do you think it was exciting?"

Susan smiled. "I was a police officer for a long time. I have seen many men like those. They are usually very weak. They were not scary."

"But they wanted to kill you!"

"No they didn't. They had no plan to kill me. They only wanted to delete that video," said Susan.

"But it was my fault. I put you in danger. I am so sorry." Lily still felt bad.

Susan laughed and put her hand over Lily's.

"You know, retirement is very boring. I enjoyed the action. It made me feel much younger. I want to say thank you!"

"Well, I think you were very brave," said Lily. "I wouldn't be so brave."

"I don't agree," said Susan. "I think you could do very well. You found out I was still in the hotel. So then the police got Luigi and he told them where to find Marco and James. The police were pleased.

They had been looking for James for a long time."

"Yes. That was good. The police have Marco, James, Robert and Luigi now," said Lily.

"Maybe you should be a policewoman," said Susan, laughing. "You would be very good."

Lily laughed too. "I'll think about it."

THANK YOU

Thank you for reading Adventure in Rome. (Word count: 6,068) We hope you enjoyed it. Other books in the City Thriller series are Trouble in Paris, and Danger in Seattle.

There are quizzes about this book on our free study site I Talk You Talk Press EXTRA. http://italk-youtalk.com

If you would like to read more graded readers, please visit our website http://www.italkyoutalk.com

Other Level 2 graded readers include
Andre's Dream
A Passion for Music
Christmas Tales
Danger in Seattle
Don't Come Back
Finders Keepers...
Marcy's Bakery
Men's Konkatsu Tales
Salaryman Secrets!
Stories for Halloween
The Perfect Wedding
The House in the Forest
The School on Bolt Street
Train Travel

Trouble in Paris
Women's Konkatsu Tales

ABOUT THE AUTHOR

I Talk You Talk Press is a Japan-based publisher of language textbooks, graded readers and language learning/teaching resources.

Our team is made up of highly experienced language teachers and translators, who have all studied at least one additional language to an advanced level.

This experience enables us to design our materials from the perspective of both the teacher and the learner. We consult with both teachers and language learners when designing our textbooks and graded readers, and test our materials extensively in the classroom before publication.

We are a fast-growing press, and currently publish graded readers for learners of English. We publish new graded readers monthly.

www.ingramcontent.com/pod-product-compliance
Lightning Source LLC
Chambersburg PA
CBHW022349040426
42449CB00006B/791